KIRSTIE ROWSON

Covered In Gold Confetti

GW00499990

Cover painting and design by Kirstie Rowson.

First edition published in 2020.

ISBN: 978-1-8380505-5-9

www.ifindoubtcreate.co.uk

This book was professionally typeset on Reedsy.
Find out more at reedsy.com.

Contents

Forward

There's no escaping the fact that I wrote these poems in the aftermath of losing my brilliant nephew, Ben to leukaemia. I've never written poetry before but in the months after he left us, I found fragments falling into my mind. Words that started to express my grief. Words that often didn't make any sense at all. It felt like the trauma was too big, too overwhelming to articulate so my mind had to break it into pieces. I wrote down whatever words came to me and over the months revisited them and found myself shaping them into short poems. It had never occurred to me that I would write poetry. It felt like Ben had given it to me as a gift to comfort me. As somewhere to 'go', to feel love when the grief floored me.

Over time, the poems became about all sorts of other subjects too. I realised they were starting to articulate feelings I had about love, loss, break ups, connection, creating, nature, therapy, kindness. They allowed me to express all kinds of things.

The poems within are in no particular order. Some feel finished and some feel abandoned but I hope some of the words resonate with you and maybe bring some comfort or encourage you to write down your fragments too.

With love,
Kirstie

Rest

Pull the blanket of cloud
Down from the sky
Let it wrap around your tired bones
Curl on cushions
Turn the volume down
And dream in muted tones
For tomorrow
The music will return
Loud and beating through your chest
Tomorrow
Will be in technicolour
But first a day of rest

When The Clocks Go Back

I am woken
Broken in two
Snapped
The clocks have fallen back in the night
One more hour
Knowing he is gone
And I am neither here nor there
Caught in the hands
Between ground and air

Translation

I'm sorry I'm late
Let me translate

I can't leave the house
I'm slumped on the floor
Thrown down by grief
In a heap by the door

I can't lift my head
I wanted to call
On second thoughts
I don't think I'll make it at all

Jam Jar

I handed myself to you
The only one
Who could open a jam jar with ease
And as you opened up my mind
Everyone else who tried before
Looked on in disbelief

Ribbons

You make me see colours
You make me see clearly
You make me honest
You take away my stutter
You make me see myself
You pull my story from me
Like a magician
Pulling ribbons from my mouth

Autumn

The autumn came
And carried you further from me
Colours changed with my grief
The leaves fell to the floor
Curling and brittle
Swept and spun away by the cold winds of winter

On the frozen path
I felt you walking beside me
We watched the seasons slide away
And I decided to stay with you
Warm in the summer
Where you reached for my hand

Sparks

I saw them
Sudden sparks
I'm sure I saw them
And yet my mind returns to dark
And I find I am blind
In this vast, forbidding place
Desperate for comfort
Lost in this space
When sudden wild flashes
Ignite into flames
Illuminate the shadows
Setting me ablaze
Neon pink, glowing
Lights rising and turning
Effortless, vibrant
Bright and burning

Safe

And I held myself in my arms
Safe and soundly sleeping

Hug

Our shoulders
Close and curved
Warm like sand to the sea
Shifting with the tide
Settling in our shapes
We move and replace
Surrounding and becoming
One another's space

Weeping In The Street

I spend time standing still on pavements
With tears rolling, strangers strolling by
With a flicker of their eye
Why is she crying?
Why is that grown woman weeping in the street?
I look at them square in the face
Unashamed, I confess
I'm bereft
Lost and left
I am crumpled, cheated
I am beaten and defeated
My feet stuck on the path
Soaked in sorrow
And tomorrow I'll do the same
I'll be here again
With tears rolling, strangers strolling by
Until the flicker of their eye
Slowly subsides

Don't I Know You

Just an accidental glance
And now we can't stop staring
Red with recognition
Well beyond caring
"I know you", I venture
"I mean
I've known you"

We say it all in that look
Did we have other minds?
Did we have different faces?
Your words are like mine
"Now I know", you venture
"You, my love
Are a home from home"

Nature

You grow around me
Like nature around an old house
Reaching around my curves
Sewing touch and planting words

You

There is resonance
In your countenance
And as the silence settles
The only sound
Is the vibration
Of you and me

In The Dust

It pulls me to my edges
Drags me by my heels across the floor
Empties my heart in the dust
And dumps me by the door

I'm in pieces on the ground
With dirt on my face, dirt in my hair
But in the midst of the mess
Dust catches light in the air

How can there be beauty
Moved by my slow and laboured breath
But by breathing, I can picture you
As love floods my empty chest

Gold

As I am unravelled
You spin me into gold

Feather

There was a feather on the train today
On the seat next to me
A small white feather
Out of place
As if he had seen my morning anger
Sat himself down next to me
And said, "Lighter Auntie K,
Be lighter."

Murmuration

I am carried up by threads held in their beaks
Held by my wrists, held by my feet
And released
Lightly circling amid the murmuration
Twisting, turning, tumbling with the starlings
I trace your name in the blue
The letters like symbols calling me to you
And we are high
Cradled by the sky

Spoons

We reshape gently
Limbs settling
One by one
By one by one
Quietly rearranging
Like spoons in a drawer

Drifting

My heart listens
To your softly spoken words
And unfolds itself like a sheet
Held aloft and shaken over head
Drifting down gently
To lay lightly on the bed

Shame

Please don't shame me
When I tell you I love you
Just because
You could never say the words

My love is rare and uncovered
Daring and kind
Vulnerable
My love is mine

So do not even think to shame me
When you could never find the words to tell me
Because by saying that I love, I walk defiantly
To the very edges of my poetry

Flames

You break me into flames
Into sparks
They catch in my hair
Catch in my heart
Set me ablaze
Light up the dark

Follow

The voice tells me to follow its poetry
Hold out your hands, it whispers kindly
Catch my falling shapes
Hold onto my letters
Come, follow me
Tie my words together with string
Trust my lines
Let me take your weight
I'm a raft in the flood
Come away with me
And let's float fiercely down the river
To a place of peace

Drawn

I sketch us in pencil, face to face
Trace our lines and curves
Drawn to draw you
Not only drawn, compelled
I scribble your hands in my hair
Outline your shoulders
And draw my arms across your back
Crafted on paper, gently held

Tell Me Stories

And I repeat
And repeat
"Tell me stories
To restore me"
Like a mantra
That will cure me

A Break Up, Two Ways

Now I know
You didn't love me
And I am cut loose
Like a glass falling from your hand

Now I know
You didn't love me
And you are cut loose
Like a glass falling from my hand

Lost

Gazing up at the inky sky
The lost girl rests
On the curve of the moon
As it rocks on the roof
Pinpointed stars gather
Drawn to the scene
Here to watch over her
And the lost girl sleeps
And the lost girl dreams

Ultramarine

I lay my face against you
Tracing your shoulder
With a brushstroke
Along the curve and angle
Round and down
Ultramarine and pink
A streak in your hair
And paint on my cheek

Soaked

And now let's talk about heartbreak
Because how can we not
We are drenched in it
Soaked and submerged
Saturated and shivering
Dragging it around with us
Flooded by desperate relief
As we wade into each other's arms

Be Still

Be still my beating mind
I borrow the poet's words
And wait for the reply
A low angered rumble
Behind my eyes
As my mind glares at me
In disbelief
Be still my beating mind
Be still

Your Move

Your move
Make it a good one
Make it butterflies
Or even better
Make it fireworks
I will dare
To look you in the eye
If you will dare
To light up the sky

Portraits

You invited me in to your home
Almost like you'd forgotten
That you never let anyone in
That you live alone
You placed your words along the hallway
And our steps echoed on the floor
As you pointed out your portraits
And opened another door

You laid the table with your stories
Offered me some wine
And we laid on the couch
Forgetting ourselves
As you enveloped me
In the arms of your history

Wolves

Now is the time for the silvery fur of wolves
To brush past the moon
For the paws of hares to scamper
Leaving their traces in the fields
And for the bears to run to the warmth of their dens
Curling in the shape of their mothers
Nestled in their layered coats
Safe from the frost and hidden from the snow

Hopeless

We are as hopeless as the night
Moving as slow as the shadows
Shifting shape across
The luminous curve of the moon
As I close my eyes
I see the stars inside
And summon the light
That blinds between us
The light that binds between us
While the sun is as far away as it can be

Shaken

Everything shook
And rearranged
Messy, disturbed
Thick with dust
Disrupted

I was left standing
Stunned
In the nonsense of it all
The silence of it all
Making no sense of it all

It was too big to fight
Too fucked up to put in any order
Speechless
My voice lost in the noise
I tried to smooth the edges

Therapy

Therapy
It won't let me clamber carelessly
Over rocks and rubble
To reach the calm on the other side
There is no other way
But to drill into my heart
And to stumble through
Shamelessly

Swimming

We have had to swim down
Down and down
Far from the shimmering surface
Back to the bed of the sea
The bed where we grew
From the sand up to the stars
Down to go up
Down to grow up

Battle

Everything has been a battle
And now's the time for peace

Return

We found our way back
We recollected
We reconnected
Like a lifetime had passed
Like it was yesterday
Like it was only tonight
We remembered the way we moved
We remembered the way we moved each other
We remembered the way we moved with each other
Like we were
Like we always had been
Like we were seen

All You Need To Know

You are worthy
Of recovery

Life Is Long

Don't think of life as short
Life stretches out
Long and languorous
In front of us
It uncurls, unfurls
Playful and mischievous
Life runs ahead
Glancing back with light in its eyes
Enticing, beckoning
Fill me with stories, it whispers
Fill me with love
See me
Really see me
Love me
Live me

The Mess

We entered into it all
With our hearts
In desperate places
How could we know
The mess was obsessed with us
How could we know
The decades it would take
To dismantle the drama

Healing

And now's the time for feeling
And now's the time for healing

Time

Time, the rearranger
Made you a stranger
Made me long for you
And your familiar heart
Made us love different faces
Made us hide in different places
When all we longed for
Was to turn back the hands
To upturn the sands
And to rearrange the pieces

Signs

It's so amazing
There are so many ways in which
You can send me signs

Starting Small

How nice would it be
To feel no fear at all
We could just feel love
Even if we're starting small

Constellations

Constellations
Are hiding in your eyes
Invitations in your mouth
Declarations of love
Are waiting for you
To come out of hiding

Threads

I dress it up with poems
With words and lines and rhymes
Carefully clothing my feelings
In knitwear and threads

But under the wool
Under the cotton and lace
Carefully concealed under layers
You make my hidden heart race

Poetry

Poetry doesn't listen to me
It can't be summoned
Or commanded
It won't obey me
Or bow down to me
The words ignore my requests
They scatter in my head
They make their own way
And I
I am impressed
For I love their wayward ways
I love their rebellious lines
Restless and unruly poems
That write themselves
Inside my mind

Fated

If I wrote a line for you
It would say
I am illuminated
Intoxicated
I am fated
To write lines for you

And the lines
Would spill into verses
And the verses would become pages
Every page a poem for you
Because I am fated
To write lines for you

Lockdown

The streets fell silent
And the trees
And the seas
Were left in peace
The skies were clear
The air was calm
And the people
Took the chance to be

Three Dimensions

When this is all over
When you can come over
No more screens
No more Zoom
Just us in three dimensions
In the same room
Lying like spoons
Settled in shapes all afternoon
And there we will stay
Stirring into the night
Whispering sweet somethings
As dark turns to light

Rebellion

I held rebellion in my hands
And showed it to the stars
This is me, I whispered
And the night sky glittered

Shaded

We are shaded by the trees
Resonating
Almost like we're meditating
Footsteps fall amidst the leaves
Slowly you tune into me
As we become a frequency

Salt

I dream of the sea
And I drift and drift deeper into the reverie
Back and forth, I am with the waves
The salt water rising up to save me
Twisting and smoothing my hair
Making gold with the glare of the sun
It runs its soothing hands across my limbs
And the rhythm of the tide speaks and sings

Just One

You may be just one twinkling star
In a distant constellation
But you don't know how transfixed I am
By your illumination

Spirals

In my mind
We are entwined
Your arm settles on my side
And we hide
In spirals of slumber

Winter Coat

As his hands rest on my shoulders
I feel the weight that went before
Slide off my back like a winter coat
Falling gently to the floor

Tempest

As the rain beats down on your tired skin
And the shadowed clouds come rolling in
Hold your nerve, my love
Turn your face to the sky
Stare into the wild
Look the storm in the eye
Keep your heart steady
And you will find
In the midst of the tempest
The stillness hides
And there is life in the rain
When the storm subsides

The Story

I took the book down from the shelf
And gently blew the dust away
Brushing the sadness from myself
I found the words still on the page
The story that ended in tragedy
Had only been partly written
I picked up my pen and looked at the sun
And tried to get back to living

Covered In Gold Confetti

The balloon popped
And suddenly
We were covered in gold confetti
Shocked into silence
Lit by shining circles
Looking at each other with wide eyes
You told me you needed to calm your heart
And then we laughed
Golden circles in our hair
Like a thousand tiny halos

I found those glittering discs
In the days to come
In my bags, in my clothes
Like you had left them there for me, to comfort me

Weeks went by and I was walking down an alley
That led to who knows nowhere
No longer able to recognise the world
Unable to raise my gaze from the ground

And there they were beneath my feet
Glittering in the dust and dirt
Waiting to greet me
A hundred pieces of gold confetti
I stopped and stood and stared
Weeping in the street
Unable to believe
You had laid this golden carpet at my feet
A magic trick, a prank, a treat
Just as you would do
Goodness, how I miss you
My brilliant nephew

Printed in Great Britain
by Amazon